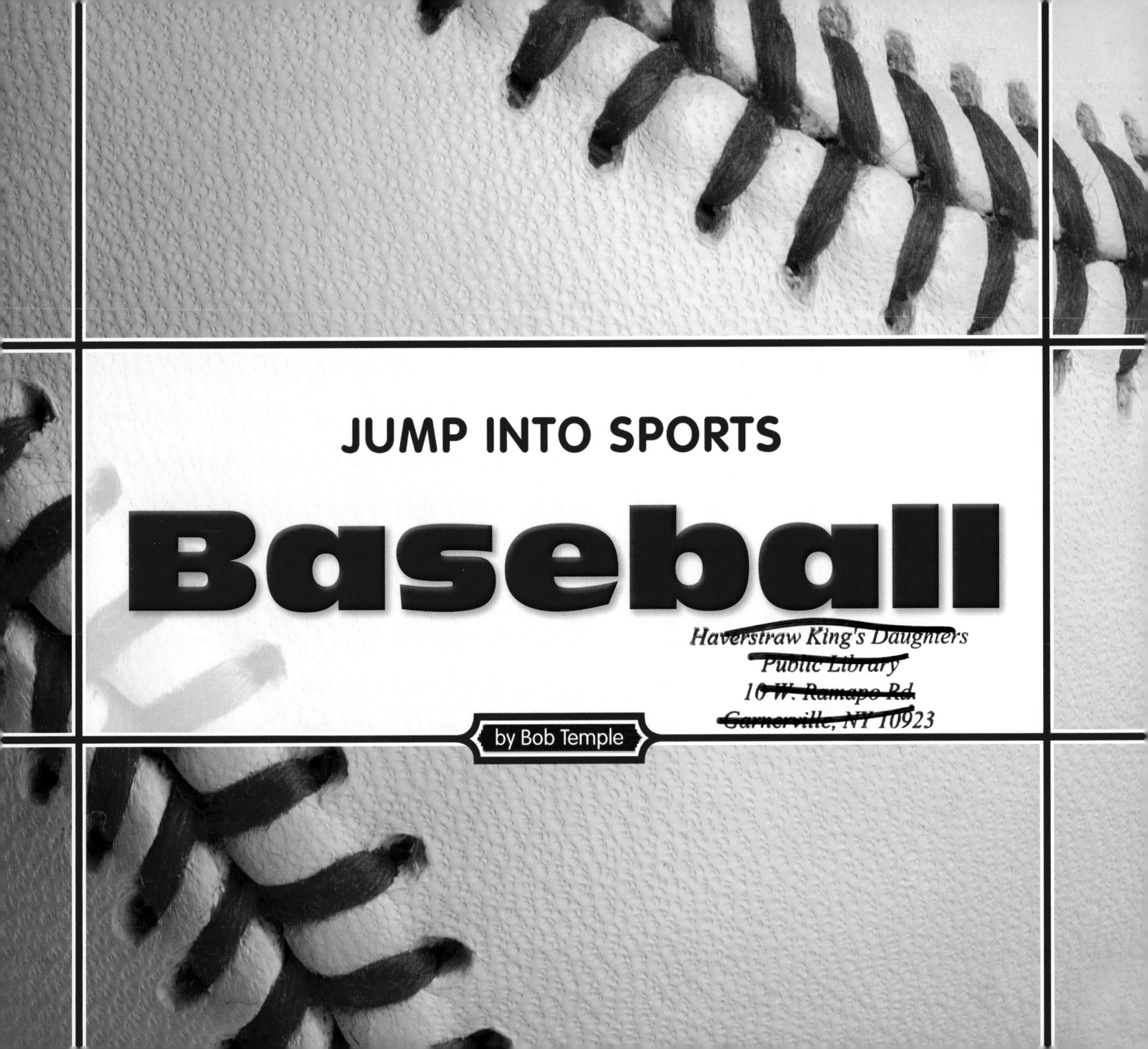

JUMP INTO SPORTS

Baseball

by Bob Temple

Grab your **glove** and your bat! It is time to play baseball.

Baseball players use **equipment** such as helmets, bats, and balls.

The game is played on a baseball field. Sometimes the field is called a **diamond**.

A **base** is at each corner of the diamond.

Nine people play for each team. One team is in the field, and the other team is at bat.

Teams often have extra players. The players take turns.

There are many different positions in the field. Some players play near the bases. They are called **infielders**. The players behind the infielders are called **outfielders**.

Baseball players must be able to catch the ball well.

The **pitcher** pitches the ball. The catcher squats behind **home plate** to catch the ball.

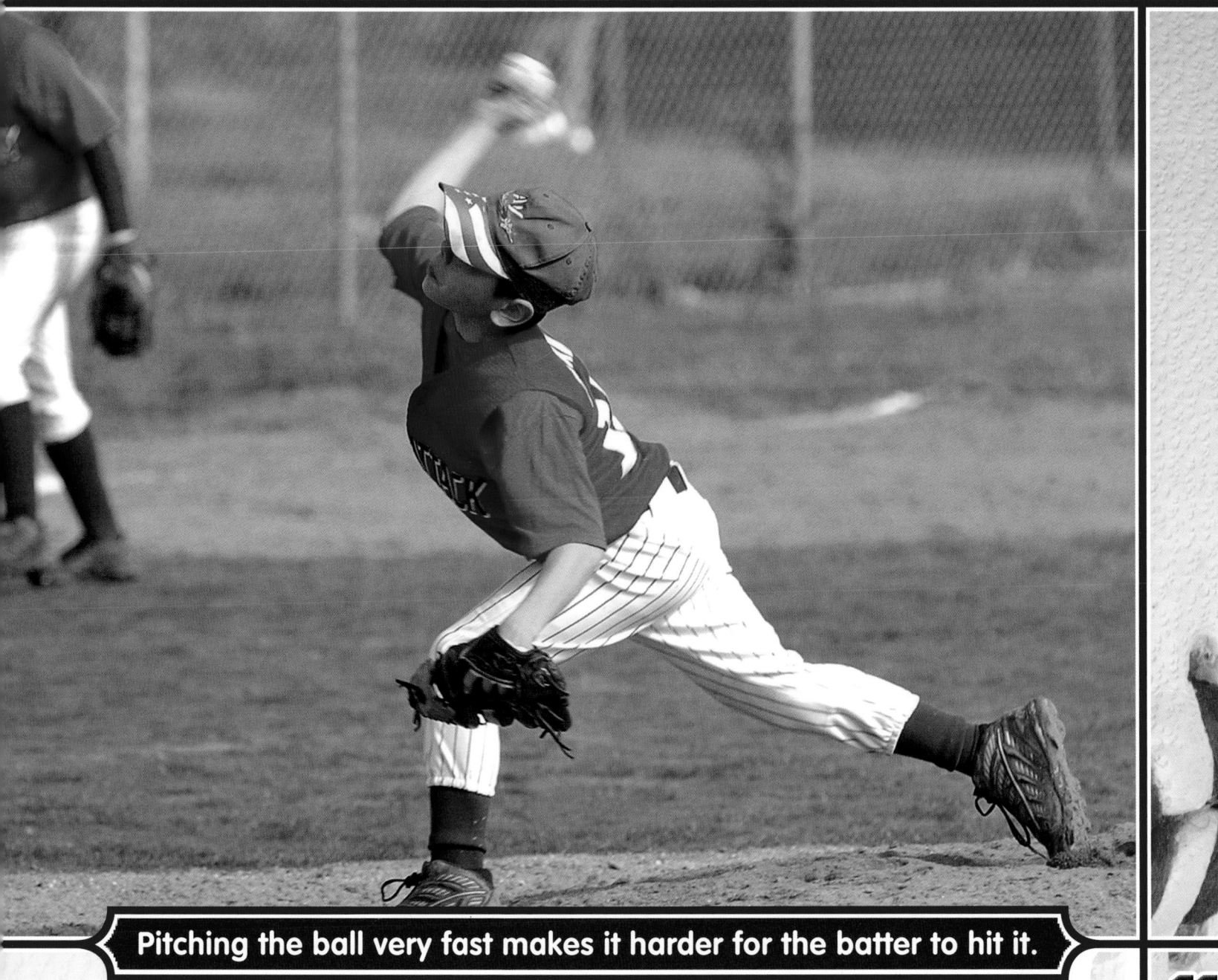

Pitching the ball very fast makes it harder for the batter to hit it.

The batter stands next to home plate. The batter tries to hit the ball to get on base.

When a batter swings and misses the ball, it is called a **strike**.

When the ball is hit, the team in the field tries to catch it. If a player catches the ball before it hits the ground, the batter is **out**.

Some players dive to catch the ball!

Fielders can also get the batter out by throwing the ball to the first baseman before the batter gets there.

The batter must reach first base before the other team throws the ball there.

The batting team tries to get around the bases and touch home plate. When a player does this, it counts as a **run**.

Some players slide into a base.

The batting team bats until it has three outs. Then the other team gets its turn to bat!

Baseball is a fun team sport.

Glossary

base (BAYSS): A base is at each corner of the baseball diamond. Players must run around the diamond and touch each base to score a run.

diamond (DYE-mund): A diamond is the part of the baseball field made up of first base, second base, third base, and home plate. Sometimes a baseball field is called a diamond.

equipment (ih-KWIP-munt): Equipment are the things used to play a sport. Baseball equipment includes gloves, bats, and balls.

glove (GLUV): A glove is a covering for the hand. A baseball player wears a glove to help him catch the ball.

home plate (HOME PLAYT): Home plate is the base the catcher squats behind to catch pitches. Each batter stands next to home plate when it is his turn to bat.

infielders (IN-feeld-erz): Infielders are the players who play near the bases. Infielders must be able to catch the ball and throw it very quickly.

out (OWT): An out is when a batter is no longer able to run or bat. A team must get three outs before it can bat.

outfielders (OWT-feeld-erz): Outfielders are the players who play behind the infielders. Outfielders try to catch the ball before it hits the ground.

pitcher (PICH-ur): A pitcher throws the ball for the batter to hit. A pitcher stands in the middle of the baseball diamond.

run (RUN): A run is when a person touches home plate. At the end of the game, the team with the most runs is the winner.

strike (STRIKE): A strike is when a batter swings and misses, or the ball is pitched in the strike zone. After the third strike, the batter is out.

To Find Out More

Books

B Is for Baseball: Running the Bases from A to Z.
San Francisco, CA: Chronicle Books, 2009.

Grippo, Daniel. *Playing Fair, Having Fun: A Kid's Guide to Sports and Games.* St. Meinrad, IN: One Caring Place, 2004.

Jacobs, Greg. *The Everything Kids' Baseball Book.*
Cincinnati, OH: Adams Media Corporation, 2006.

Nevius, Carol. *Baseball Hour.* Tarrytown, NY:
Marshall Cavendish, 2008.

Web Sites

Visit our Web site for links about baseball:
childsworld.com/links

Note to Parents, Teachers, and Librarians: We routinely verify our Web links to make sure they are safe and active sites. So encourage your readers to check them out!

Index

About the Author

In his long writing career, **Bob Temple** has been a sportswriter and an award–winning author. He has written dozens of books for young readers. Bob owns a development house that specializes in creating children's educational books. He lives with his family in Minnesota.

On the cover: Baseball players use balls, gloves, and bats.

Published by The Child's World®
1980 Lookout Drive • Mankato, MN 56003-1705
800-599-READ • www.childsworld.com

ACKNOWLEDGMENTS
The Child's World®: Mary Berendes, Publishing Director
The Design Lab: Design and production
Red Line Editorial: Editorial direction

PHOTO CREDITS: Jerome Skiba/iStockphoto, cover; Jim Jurica/iStockphoto, cover; PhotoDisc, 2, 10; Daniel Bendjy/iStockphoto, 3; Big Stock Photo, 5, 7, 11; Joseph Abbott/iStockphoto, 9; Jeff Thrower/Shutterstock Images, 13; Rob Friedman/iStockphoto, 15, 17; Carolyn Kaster/iStockphoto, 19; Jim Kolaczko/iStockphoto, 21

Printed in the United States of America in Mankato, Minnesota.
November 2009
F11460

LIBRARY OF CONGRESS CATALOGING-IN-PUBLICATION DATA
Temple, Bob.
 Baseball / by Bob Temple.
  p. cm. — (Jump into sports)
 Includes index.
 ISBN 978-1-60253-367-7 (library bound : alk. paper)
 1. Baseball—Juvenile literature. I. Title. II. Series.
 GV867.5.T46 2010
 796.357—dc22   2009030584

All sports carry a certain amount of risk. To reduce the risk of injury while playing baseball, play at your own level, wear all safety gear, and use care and common sense. The publisher and author take no responsibility or liability for injuries resulting from playing baseball.